P9-AFD-899

Ode to the Chinaberry Tree
and Other Poems

Ode to the Chinaberry Tree

and Other Poems

James Applewhite

Louisiana State University Press
Baton Rouge and London
1986

Designer: Albert Crochet
Typeface: Linotron Palatino with Zaph International
Typesetter: Moran Colorgraphic
Printer: Thomson-Shore, Inc.
Binder: John Dekker & Sons

Publication of this book has been supported by a grant from
the National Endowment for the Arts in Washington, D.C., a
federal agency.

Grateful acknowledgment is made to the following publica-
tions where some of these poems previously appeared: *An-
taeus; Blue Unicorn; Caesura; Cardinal; Carolina Quarterly; Interna-
tional Poetry Review; Ironwood; Kentucky Poetry Review;
Ploughshares; Poems for the Dead*, ed. Greg Kuzma, Best Cellar
Press; *Poetry; Poetry, Now; Poetry Review; Poets in the South;
Southern Humanities Review; Southern Review; Virginia Quarterly
Review.*

LIBRARY OF CONGRESS CATALOGING IN PUBLICATION DATA

Applewhite, James.
  Ode to the chinaberry tree and other poems.
  I. Title.
PS3551.P6703   1986   811'.54   85-19707
ISBN 0-8071-1298-4
ISBN 0-8071-1299-2 (pbk.)

Contents

I

Jonquils   3
Barbecue Service   4
Collards   5
A Catalog of Trees   6
Marriage Portrait   8
Earth Lust   10
Tear's Ore   11
Road Down Home   12
A Change of Light   13
My Uncle's Parsonage   14
The Advisors   16
How to Fix a Pig   18
Refuges   20
River House   21
Greene County Pastoral   22

II

A Shoreline Consciousness   27
The Falling Asleep   28
The Story of the Drawer   29
A Dream of War   30
Bare Words   31
Creek Sestina   32
Ode to the Chinaberry Tree   34
Fictional Family History   38
A Leaf of Tobacco   40
Field's Child   41
The Presences   42
For W. H. Applewhite   44

Quitting Time   50

The Table   51

The Morning After   52

She   53

The Artesian Well   54

Southern Voices   55

I

Jonquils

At the ruined homestead in spring,
Where armatures of honeysuckle,
Baskets of weed-wire, sprawl over
Old rows, twine up fruit trees,
Where poison oak thicker than adders chokes about
Stones of a hearth—a broken altar—
The jonquils have risen. Their yellows gather
On sea-colored stems. The frilled bells
Face in all directions, with a scattering of general
Attention toward the sun: now gone, yet source
Of their butter, their gold, this lidded day—
As if sunlight broken in pieces were
Rising from the earth. Like
Bright women abandoned in the wilderness.

Barbecue Service

I have sought the elusive aroma
Around outlying cornfields, turned corners
Near the site of a Civil War surrender.
The transformation may take place
At a pit no wider than a grave,
Behind a single family's barn.
These weathered ministers
Preside with the simplest of elements:
Vinegar and pepper, split pig and fire.
Underneath a glistening mountain in air,
Something is converted to a savor: the pig
Flesh purified by far atmosphere.
Like the slick-sided sensation from last summer,
A fish pulled quick from a creek
By a boy. Like breasts in a motel
With whiskey and twilight
Now a blue smoke in memory.
This smolder draws the soul of our longing.

I want to see all the old home folks,
Ones who may not last another year.
We will rock on porches like chapels
And not say anything, their faces
Impenetrable as different barks of trees.
After the brother who drank has been buried,
The graveplot stunned by sun
In the woods,
We men still living pass the bottle.
We barbecue pigs.
The tin-roofed sheds with embers
Are smoking their blue sacrifice
Across Carolina.

Collards

Green hens perching the pole
  Of a row, concentric wings
Fly you down into soil.

You catch the rain like rings
  Where a pine stump tunnels
Time backward down roots' seasonings.

If roots rot to dark channels
  Mining the forest, your fiber
Threads grease in the entrails

Of families, whose bodies harbor
  Scars like rain on a hillslope,
Whose skin takes sheen like lumber

Left out in the weather. Old folk
  Seem sewed together by pulp
Of your green rope and smoke

From the cook fires boys gulp
  For dinner along roads in winter.
Collards and ham grease they drop

In the pot come back as we enter
  The house whose porch shows a pumpkin.
This steam holds all we remember.

Sweet potatoes clot in a bin,
  Common flesh beneath this skin
Like collards. Grainy-sweet, kin.

A Catalog of Trees

A shiftlessness takes over.
Big brittle leaves like leather
Book bindings ring when I kick them.
I shuffle shoe-top deep in crusty hickories,
In sycamores biggest of all, curled, balled,
Tulip poplars where a hill
Under the straight tree trunks looks
Covered in shoemaker scraps. But not soft—
Crisped like bacon or cracklings.
From lard, that I haven't
Seen rendered in thirty-five years. Sycamore
Boles as if giraffes in white-on-white
Color the air like chalk. Air down
The hillslope has this milk-of-magnesia
Whitening as if a whiff of woodsmoke
From the fire going out
Seventy-one years ago. The ditch trickle
Glitters with rust in an odor
Of brightness, as from wash on a line,
When wind spanks the sheets like flags.
Air under trees seems always rotting
To cleanliness but this time carries a cabin
Now invisible, Model T frame by the spring,
One Mason jar covered unbroken
By water, and letters on the beech *Paul
Calahan Dan Calahan* under 1911
By an arrow toward *brooke*. A woman
Up the next-door hillslope is buried
With a stone—proper one with lettering—
The others, maybe slaves or just men
Marked with irregular found boulders
Heading the hollows under
Periwinkle. But the open slope with
Chalk light like a December morning in 1911
Is closer, over-exposed snapshot
With only the figures and cabin missing
The thing they did there, carving
Made seriously, letters on a line,

Cut deep, and the date there too,
So their mother would remember.
The light of her seeing seems this
Smoke white purer than brightness.
A Mason jar curved
Under water lets a wheel rim
Turn back to red
Of clay, brown of loam.

Marriage Portrait

Nowhere else does screened porch wire
Gray the light so steadily, do moths
Circle bulbs at noon, pecan leaves wave
As in a paperweight's fluid. Here is
Childhood's landscape, glassed in a frame.

Caught in this jewel focus, the one
Bright place squeezes water from our eyes.
I pose as the little master, apple
Of an eye, who reads, spins tales for brother.
You are the lovely outsiders' daughter,

Blond and patronized. You mouth "yes ma'am."
We skip down streets holding hands
In the yellow pinafore, knee britches—
Buildings, porches, enormous with shadow.
This says spicery from houses with pickles,

This is the world of mysterious feelings
Whose echo comes through the bedroom door:
The keys, the shortbread, small hands held,
An outgrown glove that seems a doll's.
A Europe of grown-ups far as the sky.

We look back now from that other country
Of secrets, overcoats, canes, prophylactics—
At a home town preserved in preciousness
Like peaches sealed in a Mason jar.
The rooms of that house which was houses

And rooms held in a different knowledge:
Dreams of flying, books that enclosed us
Whole days pavemented by sun.
The large space of staircases during a rain.
Innocence of violets. The cat's ruff, silver.

Trees of ordinary height made those
Summers mountainous. One cavernous hall
Kept the Roles in a trunk of treasures:
Paper silk hat, champagne slippers.
The two still try on costumes—high heels

Sharpening her steps beside his clumsy sword.
We see it a playhouse but cannot part.
As twilight mixes with perennial sun,
We recede from our vision. Like dolls gone gray.

Earth Lust

Sirened by a wind, we who belong
Here go out picking or digging, drawn
By berries past purple: the blisters' strong
Skins along the stems of thorn.
We who rupture these sweets with the tongue
Have suffered the ticks', the chiggers' penalties,
Can see beneath the three-leaved spray
To a poison inside our own bodies.
It boils up, answering the ivy's oil.

I am called again to a homestead's soil
Deep in woods, where periwinkle spread
In a green counterpane over the dead
Is irresistible. I have to go dig
Where vines and spiderwebs bind my head
Till I am dizzy in the heat, lose control,
Grab up all I can carry in a roll:
Like a live blanket to make my own bed.
Ivy-coil fangs my arms and legs.

We southerners must survive an embrace
Of briars, a thirst for a touch of earth
Too rough for love. For us born here, a poisonous
Juice scalds both sides of the fence of skin.
The soil is extended family, larger twin,
Relative forgotten in trees as the split rails
Rot down, till only periwinkle calls
Some son back to the hug that stings—
Past snake's skin, the blackberry strings.

Tear's Ore

Water of the cornea—
Quartz ore sungold veined—
A soprano piano
Chimes your innocence
Icily. Pine green hushes
The cabin, river beyond
Runs time's pig iron.
Raw clay landings
Current her tresses.
A Pamlico matinee
Rises, cinema that sunk her
Like oxide. Roan blood,
You muddy the light. Cypress
Swamps muck your brunette roots.
Antebellum woman
In a wreck underwater, your
Red hair released by the diver
Fans above treasure.
I bubble in my helmet
In the octopus' embrace.
Iron, iron, I taste you in water.
Time drowns ships, their chests
Of silks. Masts, the wheel,
Her floating hair a ghostly shimmer.

Road Down Home

Out of range of the classical station, I enter
Country music bawling from Tarboro:
Cheating and endless loves, whiskey, whiskery lips—
So Joe Speight splitting down 264
In his boat of a Chrysler might be
My father in his outboard, plowing the new flood,
The beginning waters—when Red Hill was solitary Ararat.
Still it is similar. Radio's wails like wild dogs baying
Along bends of that old river back to Nineveh. Silver air.
Log barns with pediments tilting seem
Tumuli projecting from an ancienter landscape.
The mirroring I remember about his boat
Lies ponded from recent rain: openings
Into a moonlighted Atlantis
Where the barbed wire's stringers,
Over their heads in currents of the wild dogs' cry,
Left these lines of iron
Now passing through the hearts of timber trees.
In a ditch, the circle of a clearing.
Blue silhouetted with a cabin.
Owl's whoop staring. Stone moon.

A Change of Light

Where were the live clouds for a while?
    Where was the white wet light, that depth
Of head and height and field of sky that shone
    Like sea by berg? Their herding, ancestral
Complacency, their nodding over shadow, their sense
    That death was part, like rain, a hole or tear
In veil but not the blackening curtain of nothing—
    Where had it gone? I hadn't consciously missed
That countryside of lives in sky connected
    Like the villages and roads down slopes and
Up the farther mountain past the thatched,
    Grimm Brothers roofs you take in at a glance
Until I felt it back. Till Jack walked in
    A radiant air of harp and goose and giant
Fell on his blundering rump in rain and thunder.

My Uncle's Parsonage

His watch chain looped golden nowhere
In air of the mill town. Shrubbery,
Head-high bubbles leafily guarding recollection—
Up steps to the parlor and the puzzle—
Materialized uncertainly, in connection with
The streets as I remembered. German
Shepherds now only dog-sized, not
Polar bear monuments half out of National Geographic
Frisked the one field promising
With grapevine ruin, broom sedge on ditch edge
Like bronze piano strings. He sang
At the mirror, beard still blue behind the razor,
Hymned his deep patience:
With crook-kneed walk and cane,
High chair before elevated desk in the study—
Old man, precocious child—in a room
Of biblical gilt, leather and vellum: tomes
Like tombstones, of no earthly use save to the soul.

Sick, he visited the sick, methodical
Methodist, incurably addicted to the alcoholic
Brakeman's repentances and relapses, till a whole
Load of logs from that Seaboard Railway flatcar
Pressed a last breath dead dry.
S. E., Seymour Esmond, jaw propped firmly
At the folds by ministerial collar:
Backing up your Chevrolet with head unturned,
Militarily formal, you never collided.

We put away your weeks of Sunday suits. Now that
Closet door swings open. But where
In this drugstore town, among Kiwanians
And mill hands, past signs for seed corn and tractors,
Is a soul to remember?
Your pin-striped figure is turning each corner,
Too nimble with cane for full view.
Your weight is a burden you carry like Atlas.
Blue steel spring beyond peripheral vision,

You show finer under tension.
Your watch still ticking in a room
Loops its chain around me,
Inheritance of thought, goldening air between
Your house that I know but cannot find, and
These streets where I walk, and you are not.

The Advisors

Throned on the piled treads, tired,
I'd sit like a prince with his advisors,
Orange drink for sundown. What a cast of characters.
Bill Davis damned if he'd take any shit
Since the war, when he'd carried a BAR.
And him the lightest man in his whole unit.
Ralph, ex-Marine, washing his hands in gasoline.
Rabbit-toothed James with his country guitar.

With grease guns on fittings, we fired.
We broke loose bead from truck tire rim
With wedges pounded in. Our hired
Hands felt the pressure hose heave
When blasting country mud from underneath fenders.
With kerosene stinging our skin, the spanners
Too hot to handle, we sighed for night, when we were free.
One girl was never enough if they were me.

Ralph had fed his black market Scotch
One more time to the Australian nurse,
Who wouldn't come across. Then Alice
Drove up for gas, and Ralph polished glass
Over her dress back almost to her crotch
So I wobbled with laughter on my column of rubber.
As couples in pairs drifted to Rooster's for beer,
I weighed father's coins in my pocket, felt myself heir.

Counselors who'd spent their time, they knew
Better now. The thing was to know that I was rich.
My father owned the station. If I got an itch . . . .
You could have gone off just then I said.
Shit boy. You don't know my Jen. When you're married . . . .
I saw the American heads on a patch in New Guinea.
The Japs, Ralph said, had stuck their dicks in their mouths.
Time flies, he said. Look at these moths.

Just as I was closing, Bill came back with a Bud,
Hair still wet, white shirt. I been
Meaning to ask I said. Ever get it in
With the teacher in the girdle? Yeah. Funny
Thing is, there on my knees with a hard on
Is what I remember. See before I go to sleep.
I rolled home each rubber round of that throne,
Both hands shepherding treads. Flock of black sheep.

How to Fix a Pig

(as told by Dee Grimes)

Take a piece of tin that's
Blowed off a barn in a storm.
Pile little limbs and good chunks
Of hickory on top. Get the fire going
While you're finishing the pit.
Hickory burns orange, then blue.
Dig deep enough to hide a flat-bottomed
Creek boat. Put bars across the top
Closer together than the ones in a jail.
Flop the split pig skin side down
So his eyes won't watch you.
Take a little hit from the bottle in your pocket.
When you've got good coals,
Spread 'em out under him with
A flat-ended shovel. Pretty soon
The steam starts. Douse on the vinegar
And pepper. First time you sniff him,
You start to get hungry. But you can't rush a pig.
Eat that cold chunk of corn bread
You brought from the house in a greasy paper bag.
When that vinegar and wood ashes smoke starts rising,
And blowing in a blue wind over fields,
It seems like even the broom straw
Would get hungry. But you got to stand it
At first. It comes from down home, from
When they cured tobacco with wood, and ears of corn
Roasted in ashes in the flue.
The pig was the last thing. The party
At the looping shelter when the crop was all in.
The fall was in its smell,
Like red leaves and money.
So when you can't stand it, turn up the rib side.

If you didn't get started before light,
You may be finishing after dark.
The last sparks look at you red from underneath,
Like the pig's eyes turned into coals, but forgiving.
When the whole thing's finally so brown

And tender it near 'bout
Falls to pieces when you move it,
Slide it every bit into the pan.
They're waiting to chop it up at the house.
And they going to wonder one more time
Why a pig don't have no ribs when it's done.

Refuges

Black River Shell, you
    Rescued from peril
Of the road. Your hands knew
    Innocence's distress, curl
Wet with sweat, black bomb
    Buick immobile with lost
Belt. Our car's hot tomb
    Opened to your roadside host
Of delicacies: cheese nabs,
    Orange drinks like honeysuckle
Summers, chrome from cabs
    And their hubs, tire-change struggle
Like classical drama remembered.
    Wartime nights of sixteen,
Your easy moments rendered
    Their profit. The trusted Marine
Reclaimed his restored jalopy.
    I mailed the check to Black
River Shell. All were happy.
    Bread on the waters comes back.
Your name shines darkly
    As the bombed harbor's peril
In one family's history:
    Pearl in the black shell.

River House

Linwood, old lawyer, no sermons like your brother's
For you, black frames owling your eyes—
Though your hunter's legs tangled in their veins,
Feet tripped in black shoes. I remember
Your skiff on the river, still water a steel sheet.

Your chambers stood empty of everything
But books, held spaces for waiting, writing,
Where claims urged were locked with words, lamps
Hung on chains. You breathed that dust and drank.
That day a small fish flipped into our boat.

I learned of loss in your house, Linwood,
Heard consumption's breath, pine sighs needling
A cabin, inhaled cypress' knotty odor.
Heard water, water, caught crabs in shallows,
Meat deliciously white, like kisses of fishes.

The cemetery later where you last presided
Mixed masoleum columns with seafood
Odor from Salebee's. The granite pediment,
Slabs and chunks fat as jugs or pigs, defined
A pine distance where you flickered, disappeared—

Like reflection of a face in a window,
The candlelight's distortions returned
By a flawed pane. Tall and gray, you turned,
Carried on. I kept the memento of the funeral,
Nothing specified about spectres in a pine frame.

Greene Country Pastoral

I hope that Mary Alice Philips who lived
    by the river will pick new
        jonquils for the casket.

Maybe L. G. Newcomb whose four-room house
    stood in a bend of the creek road
        will come with a fist of forsythia.

I wish the girls and boys I knew, from creekside and
    mule lot, from rosy broom sedge knolls,
        could start past edges of pine woods.

I think their singing and sighing might rustle
    with the needles and hush like the dove
        wings alighting on light wires

On hills far away in the country. Their preachers
    might come looking pale and fresh-shaven
        from the white inside the wooden churches.

May their sermons on sin and punishment subside,
    let them calm those waters. Let Jesus walk
        out of their words and pass among

L. G.'s crowd where they're turning the reel in the Contentnea.
    Let his face be from faces in the boats on
        the Neuse, the Pamlico, the Cape Fear.

Those who downed, let them arise.
    The white face of one from underwater
        will still these troubles. While they

Scoop up nets full of shad and cats and their
    campfire flickers more orange as the sun
        goes down, may the mules

In the fenced lots hang their heads sorrowfully
and turn their hindquarters to the wind,
one hoof scraping a corn cob.

May wind through dog fennel of the deserted
pasture sway the soft weeds just at the tips
so they touch the fence's wire.

May the sky and the land be one in evening,
the pale light a lake for the straw
and the twigs and the weeds

And fish in the reel and the horses and mules
and Mary Alice Philips and L. G.,
and Christ like a drowned man arisen.

Let the deserted house with scrolled cornices
in the grove of broken oaks with a few
jonquils spotting that shadow

Be circled like an elegy by swallows.
Let them know that she always loved them.
Let this light and these fields

Hold her spirit as naturally as a straw
basket carries the loose flowers.
Let the light in that cloud fade to stone.

May she lie at peace with the forsythia, spirea, willow
brought her by bare-footed farm girls
in my frail thoughts' pastoral.

A Shoreline Consciousness

Submerged, inarticulate, I couldn't get
My head up for air. Town seemed a pond.
I drowned in a unity with vapor. It covered
Oaks' crowns like swimmers underwater.
I suffered the helplessness of permament being,
Unable to tear my figure free. Yet woke
To a window's ice light, with hollyhock
Blossoming a hummingbird's cellophane wings.
His ice-pick bill tasted flowers like dresses.
Looking through glass, I saw the world from outside.
Apocalyptic angers swept my mind like winds.
My soldiers in their chinaberry shade were killed
When the flying dust looked old as Methuselah.

The Falling Asleep

Night after night the mountain opened, I fell
Into the world, explored those crumbling bridges
That sunk into rivers slithering with algae.

Falls from the sky, expulsions from a garden—
Is it the amniotic ocean we remember
The weightless floating in that primal circle?

I played with my cousin in grandmother's yard,
A high white fence around our sandy garden.
Only the beardy moss on an old barn's sides
Reminded us of time. Cherries hung perfectly
On a tree by the fish pond, where gold scales
Circling reflected their globes all seasons.
Where moss fuzzed wet on the boards, we hid.
Her slit's lips smiled, straight white fat.
My blue vein ticked: light like the glass
Clock case in grandmother's parlor. Then a cloud
Shadowed over, the branches in a wind like autumn's.
The doctors said my heart must be sick.
Rheumatic fever seemed a foreign country.
They cut my finger with a splinter of razor
And babies down the hall started crying together.

The Story of the Drawer

Father amazed us waving his pistol
In his story of the station nearly robbed.
The thirty-eight special—blued steel glossy
As cobras—nested near the cash register handle
With foil-pack prophylactics, quarters.
We imagined his hand with that blue-black bolt
Of lightning upraised, the drunk punks slinking
For the door while he danced his explosive fist
At ceiling and window. We looked in awe at the thing
Exposed, then slid the drawer shut, were quiet.

A Dream of War

The dreams of war pursued me for years:
Nurses with tubes in their mouths in blood-spattered
Aprons, too frantic to hear. Why was I enclosed
In the iron appliance like a woman's slipper,
A set-screw tightened into my side?
The storm of flame burned room by room.

With the oak tree shadows getting darker
Near the creek, stars' silver pins sticking in,
A humming of crickets crackled with static
In the radio-air from the far-off flashes.
Mosquitoes made an itching on my legs.
The Japanese bombed our white Pearl Harbor.

I lay like a wounded pilot on grandmother's porch.
Babs and Betsy wore uniforms of khaki paper.
Thunderbolts from Seymour Johnson
Fought each other in our innocent sky.
One crashed nearby. The motor like a boulder
Rolled through the pines, bowling them down.

Bare Words

Maimed intelligence, psyche too long
Restrained, how do we arrive in this cleft
Head cut heart, when underground there's breath
From moss by starting water? A sanction here
Shames mouth to work with labored birth of O,
Child to stammer. Lascivious slitherings, rubbery
Lubricity, we castigate. The diphthong's tropical
Fruit-surfaces (fuzzed or marbled, forbidden)
Stay a taste in the base of the tongue. Consonants
Like drops into pools of caverns echo memory.
Bat-flap plosives follow, when a fur-sizzle of
Rain sieves the screens. Love wakes these
Syllables, or nakedness, or swimming. A crack
In a door lets dark shine liquidly,
Breathe cellar's odor. Poet, comedian, child,
Palms his pencil to scrawl four letters. By walls
Of newsprint written with obscenity, we tramp
To kiss the nipple syllables with whiskey lips.

Creek Sestina

This room as in the dream seems now to bend
Toward water, aisles open from its corners' dust.
Between great cypress knees, the slick of creek
Lashes itself to slither, a shining snake.
My light is eaten by the quickening roots.
Sky I lift toward presses the darkness down.

The past of dreams and snakes won't stay down
In its burrow. Thoughts go in a line, then bend,
Curving back toward night. Tangled with roots
Of cypresses, air feels tacky with water-dust.
Jonah's craft in the belly of a snake,
His navigation moves along this creek.

We drifted away from light on slumber's creek,
An alley winding inward and softly down.
The plush of mud grew blacker than soot or snake.
A polish glimpsed ahead led to a bend
Where smell of swamp fell on our lips like dust.
The paddle opened doors through vines and roots.

We had no fear of drowning. A noose of roots
Loosened to squeeze us wetly through that creek.
The conscious house whose corners gather dust
Had rounded to liquid hallways leading down.
Below, a forest's flowings spread and bend,
Flicker and go. Succession is a snake.

A root beside the boat turned to a snake.
We sloped a maze from light to deeper roots.
Having forgotten current, stream and bend,
We missed the cool, amphibian pulse of creek:
Centered among directions leading down—
In wet without which light dries out to dust.

How did the dream return to solid dust?
The frog sees only night inside a snake.
The only white we saw was seeds' light down.
Yet serpents slithered backward into roots,
That lowest ooze moved outward in a creek,
Again we fathomed light around a bend.

A swamp uncovers snakes when we can bend
Our senses, trickles this dust of words: a creek
Whose up is down. Like that of wet or root.

Ode to the Chinaberry Tree

I

There was a time when sandpile, fence and tree
Cornered our play, bounded seeing
Between a green umbrella and its country of shadow.
Each soldier on his hill looked glassily lonely—
While each of us generaled his battle, castled his king.
Light like the glass in my window
Showed wet sand, one struggling ant.
Furiously as we'd burst our dirt clods in victories,
Send explosions wherever we'd please,
I wondered what these levelings meant,
Where the six-legged survivor went.
Our angers raged like the wind
When the peak-white head
Loomed absolute as the steeple of a preacher.
Shadow slipping over like the foot of a snail
Made the tree's crown bend;
A hollowness falling down the stairs of cloud
Grew louder, left the green light steeper.
The lawn shown pearled by hail.

II

Later, cooler, within seeing's tree,
I wondered why bodies were little and sweaty,
Why our fingers smelled sour with the berries' putty.
When we raged and roared
In lookout on the angle of the fence,
Supported by one slender board,
Our vision angeled holy wars: intense
As the nodding clouds' white anger.
Each of us commanded a field within,
Solitarily faced the danger,
Fought on an earth within the self.
Conscious in the tree of our original sin,
We entered our eyes from the sky's wide sight,
Teetered on a narrow shelf:

Fence-sitting children, helpless and mighty.
Our fury passed like the wind—
Impatience of the pure mind—
Had only the world as enemy.
Those years the clouds mountained a higher light.

III

Our lawn looked flat and dull. Father was mowing.
Sent to a house on the river,
I listened to the pine needles' water
Whisper of the place where I was going.
The light flushed muddy with my fever.
My cousin cracked a crab in the sun.
Her buttocks swelled rich
And ripe, round as melons.
Mosquitoes made my ankles ache and itch.
By the dark water I remembered father,
His mower moving like a boat on the river.
It frightened me to be only one,
Sick and separate from Teaky and Alice,
From our sight in the hard heat intense as ice
And our tree in the platinum sun.

IV

We colored pictures like the letters for words,
Sat in a circle where we'd spell
Out stories. Our crayons made marks bright as birds.
Then sometimes the teacher would be dull.
Numbers crawled like bugs on the board,
But we learned new games at recess.
Father made a swing for reward
With ploughline hung from a limb.
Alice went back and forth like a pendulum,
Streaking curves with her yellow dress.
If time at the river had muddied my light,
Still I'd pump for height under leaves

That moved, feel branches wave and the tree take flight.
The lift in a child's body believes
His dream of flying, his feeling of lightness.
We fell down arcs from steep
Sky, into gravity's lap of sleep.

V

Father had spanked me hard. Through a hole
In the fence where the ants' lines went
Yellow leaves piled on the coal
And I glimpsed his black car shiny against it
Turning over and over.
Breath sucked my throat as his black car bent,
Caught fire. I ran from the cover
Of that shade where imagining
Came easily as swinging.
He was still in the house in his chair
So I could wrestle his right arm
That never bent. It seemed a trunk
That held leaves firm in the wind's stir,
Strong shaft of our umbrella when storm
Blew alarm and mother looked drunk
With fright. If she was limitless as water,
He was the moored boat that saved us. Father.

VI

Frightened at my breathing's violence,
I brooded over ants from the fence.
I felt myself continuous with everything,
Streamed with the wet light to clouds that slid
Their shadow over houses and trees like wings.
And I was a kid little as his body,
Spanked for the sneakiness I did.
Bruise marks shadowed the perfect day
The light had cast around scenes I'd see.
Autumn began to yellow the tree.

VII

Caught within my skin, I felt a fever.
Light ran brown as I remembered the river.
White meat of mussels marked slits on Alice whenever
I'd see her. The first time my own stiff thing spit white,
The burning like a shadow on the sight
From staring at the sun scarred all the daylight.
Days went faster after that.
Soon I was restless and muscled, hurt
My friends when I'd tackle them in football
At school. I answered the call
With Alice's friend. Later I would marry.
The changing sky made everything hurry.

VIII

Chinaberry tree, our separate country,
We tenanted your green imagining.
From our flight of mind that aimed too
High, we arced in descents
You cushioned with your cotton swing.
Above the coal pile's kingdom of ants,
Your shadow and sun disguised the pure blue.
In your skin of shade, it was childhood and morning.

Fictional Family History

Southerners seem loneliest.
A wooden porch with rockers. Brothers
In the Tennessee ridge house with women
Dressed in black. One their mother.

The iron-fenced graveyard with broom sedge,
Ridged lonelier than any space else
For father, living, his new stone place
In death. Heaves of chests, her serious weeping.

Those windows had hung their crosses
Over distances, on the hills—seemed
Suspending one family in the air, to show
Explorers had discovered only vacancy:

Too much innocence in the snakes,
Mountains repetitions in mirrors,
A sky blank as Eden's. Leaves held
Sun like the Madonna with Christ,

Dumb in their ecstasy. Father
Missed a history. Lonely to the last,
Adding his body to the vast inarticulate
Which yielded deer so abundantly,

He ended. His name and sufferings
Form part of our story. Perhaps if
A preacher instead of a farmer, his buggy
Rides at all hours of the night would

Have made more sense. He just went,
Then lay down his burden. We seek the meaning.
Our loneliness is consciousness, and vice versa.
Waking to ourselves, apart from a vista

That mirrors, is the fall, where all stories
Begin. Family genes, the cloudy innocence
We cannot bear, recall this father in summers,
Raise pine torches to his wraith, charcoal

Flares on the deck, burnt sacrifice
From an heir. Empty chairs still rock
The South's wide porches. I light
This writing with tones from the dove's

Call, steam engines wailing
Far off, dull memory of a small
Town's moonlight, the unendurable
Purity of privacy. Father we thank

You for our fall as we must.
We pray you lie in your green ease
Still lonely. Better you than mother.
We murdered for lust. Her beautiful body.

A Leaf of Tobacco

Is veined with mulatto hands. The ridges extending
Along crests of the topographical map from the stem
Marking a mountainous ridge encounter wrinkles
Where streams lead down toward coastal pocosins.
This time-yellowed scrap of a partial history
Features humans driven on like mules with no reprisal.
The grit your fingers feel exploring this pungent terrain
Is fragments of a Staffordshire tea service
Buried from Sherman in fields near Bentonville.
The snuff-colored resin on the ball of your finger
Crystallized in the corners of seventy-five-year-old lips,
On the porch of a shotgun shack, as she watched her grandsons
Crop lugs on their knees in the sun. This leaf has collected,
Like a river system draining a whole basin,
The white organdy lead bullet coon dog Baptist
Preacher iron plough freed slave raped and
Bleeding dead from the lynch mob cotton
Mouth South. Scented and sweetened with rum and molasses,
Rolled into cigarettes or squared in a thick plug,
Then inhaled or chewed, this history is like syrupy
Moonshine distilled through a car radiator so the salts
Strike you blind. Saliva starts in the body. We die for this leaf.

Field's Child

Pastures look inhabited,
Like windows. Ponds turn white
As stars on a tin roof, while
Barbed wire limits the isolation.
One scene framed in fence posts,
Failing as in eyes of an aproned woman,
Is saved by a movement:
The pumpkin hound with pine
Tree brown whose bark
Colors the squirrel's fur
Quicksilver. The small boy follows.
His gun is a stick,
His whistle a star's light.
Moon's fingernail creases his path.
His memory was what
Inhabited the field: warm
Hearth brick, taste of an iron nail
In the well bucket's water. Woodsmoke
Baked into a biscuit. He breaks
Into a trot, doesn't have to whistle his dog.
The pastures where I have not yet seen him
Wait for him, broom sedge holding
Or seeming to hold the sunset
In that rosy straw, that Adam's clay.

The Presences

Again they come into being.
Long bark antlers
This granite forehead—thorns
The crown of seeing.

Steps I've staked with cedar
Lift to the wood's
High altar. I follow.

Asparagus-elongated,
Candling a cake of mulch
And granite, they celebrate
This day's birth-light.

I run through twigs and
Briars by the river. Breathe
Clean pain. Perplexities
Kindle: gray responsibilities.
This wooden route of manhood.

Great grandfather, limb
Shot off at Cold Harbor,
You died before I knew.
Why is my retreat
The treehouse of a boy?
I must stand and fight.

Candles of incorporated
Cleanliness,
Hard facts killingly
Heavy, stubborn to uproot,
Lifting definitions
Made of sunlight, water, and
Our carbon dioxide breath,
Metabolize me purely.

Dawn shapes its
Sentinels from compost, mist.
You weathered veterans
Able-bodied longer than men,
Topple with nightfall.
At the pulse of glowing,
Branch your arteries
In our eyes
Which create them.

Dark conscious blood
Though in temples of aching,
Obscuring your shining creation,
Throb this ridge into being.

For W. H. Applewhite

Everything was large to the child's eye, the peaches,
The apples and cantaloupes. Tall boards
Fenced space by the scuppernong trellis.
Sun past the shades in inch-thin shafts
Fixed motes of dust to a Brownian motion.
Bookcases hid their gilt titles behind
A partial reflection, gleamed like dim flame:
Glass clock case, foil-wrapped candy.
And ghostlier wisps, breaths of the children
A day in winter when the stove went out.
Hall floor trembled when I stepped on a board—
Signal to memory that a taste lived on,
Where a man almost eighty gave water to a boy.
His memory held an earlier era: a steamboat
To the New York fair, when soot spoiled his hat.
Horse and buggy courting, when ten miles two ways
Was a day. Baseball on smooth-packed pastures,
When he'd wait for the high hard one, inside.
We tipped in our rockers, watching the horizon,
That porch leaned into by a final sun-slant:
"Been eighty-six years and it seems like a day."

W. H. grew up in the nineteenth century,
In the two-story farmhouse on the Wilson road.
It stands today, upstairs porch railed in
Before narrow windows, their antique glass
Upright and open toward the cleanly furrows.
Their hand-blown panes show lines imperfectly,
As if miraging heat since the Civil War
Had imprinted ripples. Oaks are enormous,
Two crown-ruined by the August lightning.
Roots gnarl the yard, china-bare, sandy,
By latticed masonry, with old-fashioned roses
Not much redder than their brick-work trellis.
W. H. played by this doorstep, cranked water
From an iron pump's jaws, by the set-apart
Kitchen. He broke land in spring with a mule,
Gripping handles worn slick by callouses,

One cotton ploughline over a shoulder.
He dug gray marl near the swamp, set out
Tobacco by hand, broke the suckers and tops
Before they flowered, leaving some for seed.
Cropped the broad sand lugs, bent double
In air hot rank in his face from the rained-on
Soil. Low spots grew weeds, sandy rises
Starved the corn. Putting in tobacco worked
Everyone: great black women twined hands
Of leaves to the sticks for hanging. Log barns
Heated for curing with winter-cut wood
Were tended all night, sweet corn roasted
In coals or a pig barbecued by the looping
Shelter: pine brush on rafters of saplings.
Gray-breasted gardens grew watermelons,
Cantaloupes, squash and tomatoes. Canning
In kitchens with pots large as vats
Wrinkled aprons and skin with the steam.
Pigs were strung up from timbers in December.
Their blood steamed like ghosts in the cold.
Fat cut in books was rendered for lard,
Gut-casings scraped for sausages. Salt-cured
Hams turned a river-water color,
Sliced out shiny as planed-over pine knots.

With white church walls around him on Sundays,
Hell felt plausible in the ninety-degree heat.
Steeples warned strictly as Lot's salt wife
Across the cinder fields. He learned the returns
Of crops and seasons, closed in by miles
Which sand roads, pine barrens, swamps, made
A limit to curiosity. The stars' light,
The King James Bible and Wesley's hymns,
Traveled equivalent distances, unquestioned.
Hand-pumped organs like voices from the grave
Brought penitents to the altar while clouds went over.
After beans, boiled ham, the stillness descended.
All a man's courage and love were required

That he keep to the scriptural promise, not
Shamble behind a barn for a quick corn
Whiskey like a snake's strike in the mouth.
Grandfather's father drank in the packhouse,
Stumbled over roots his shoes wore shiny,
An example to W. H. that a fitness
Must be preserved. Later in the columned
House whose parlor held his time for childhood,
W. H. presided over our ritual repasts.
The farm sent water in five-gallon jugs,
Thanksgivings' tea and coffee made with it.
China and silver on the walnut table
Looked delicate and perfect, goblets tinkling
Ice in the water. He asked our blessing
And carved the turkey, serving a communion
In the common experience, reverently slicing
A cantaloupe like summer's explanation.
Sundays, Thanksgiving, Christmas, Easter
Were celebrated there in a heart-pine center,
A house that varnish made yellow as amber.

I interpret the rooms it windowed around us,
Read flights of birds like a seer through its panes—
Wonder at landscapes, genealogies in Bibles.
See elaborate logics drift toward mythology,
The Big-Bang cosmology an inferior Genesis.
The stars' secret is, their distances of time
And number are too vast for comprehension:
Red shift recessions in cosmic radiation
Mere fantasies for eyes within horizons.
The space-time discontinuities
Of quantum gravity puzzle the senses.
On an earth dreamed flat by our limbs,
We set up gravestones in Euclidean geometries,
Plant shafts' inscriptions by streams, where battles
Made nations, render perspectives of landscapes
Where roofless windows of Cistercian abbeys
Point arches over trees with impractical purity.

I hold to this map of simplicities arranged
By feeling, place-plan where seeing and skin
Encountered a world, knew water and sun,
Their flavors like essences, worth being born for:
Snowflakes singly for the tongue on white skied
Washerwomen days when I thought them ashes.
Cracklings from lard-rendering crusty as bread,
Ground pepper, old wood with fat rubbed in it,
Meals from ranges fed with split pine billets.
Town, you satisfied taste, met touch
To the full, a capsized boat my baptism.
Your infant is alive in the eye, in each glance
Over water, inhalation of autumn's scuppernongs.

W. H. gardened in the ground behind his house
Until his heart forbade it. But one spring,
The root-spikes of vegetables wanting to go down,
He got out his wooden handplough, opened
Two rows beneath the April clouds,
Now alone, where we'd romped by his work,
Our grandmother dead before. He came inside,
To the table where he'd served me the water,
Put his head on his arms and died,
Like a boy off to sleep before supper.
There at the cemetery—as townspeople walked
To pay last respects, Nell Overman
With shoulders held straight, Norwood Whitley
Marching courageously, Ann Louise Stanton
And her sister in their sober colors on wintry
Grass—I saw his body on a mattress
Whose ticking was the tape-striped furrows,
Whose tufting was cotton's white eyeballs from boles.
He was borne away as on wooden spokes
Shaved to fit hubs and rimmed with iron,
Saluted by mules' ears tapered like corn cobs,
By broom sedge in furled inclination,
Occupying gullies and ruts, undefeated
On clay too poor for pine seedlings.

He lay for me there on a pillow of fields,
Floated a river from the backwoods shanties
Seasoned with pine resin and kerosene.
Mother's grandfather, his arm shot off
At Cold Harbor, died before I knew.
William Henry, you were the one true
Father, the Bible-carrying walker-on-water
Of a time that escapes us, Mississippi
Flood of our cotton gins and buggies
Swept away, Klan drowned with lynchings
And coon hunts and burns from the cook stoves
And men marrying quickly again when the wife
Died in childbirth. Man like a blued steel
Stove flue for a land the cotton couldn't
Soften or tobacco draw the sting from,
You died necessarily, waved to by the riddled
Battle flag behind glass at Appomattox.
Your people ate clay, grew lean with sawed
Pines, leather-jawed with high shoes and harnesses.
Eyes of brown children soft as cotton
Saw vittles brought home from tables their mothers
Cooked for. You walked the waters of those days,
Your white shirt shone like sun on the clapboard
Steeples, your scriptural readings rung like
Their bells across fields. You were another time
I knew. I remember your boney beak,
Your apples, your bent-kneed carrying of water,
As if half-kneeling before the sanctity
Of the simplest gestures: gardening, blessing
Our potatoes, turnips, the country ham
Pungent with forests of hickories, salt
As the tears your grandfathers sowed into this soil.
The coffin that carried you away from me
Rocked like a flat-bed wagon, toward hills
Half-liquid with sun heat in a distant pasture.
The land of your corduroyed mattress moved
In a swell, you drifted toward trees like the wall

Of a wave on the horizon when a child first
Sees the sea. Your bronze box buoyed me,
Ark of a covenant on water till doomsday.

Quitting Time

Mill workers migrating
north with the four
o'clock shift from
American Tobacco
stream the road,
refugees, battered big
Plymouths and Olds
hiding rust and dirt under
pretentious fenders:
sliding and nosing toward
Roses and K-Mart toward
collards and ham hock and
a cotton tee shirt
a beer before TV—
toward a cigarette's
blue ghost and ash and
forgetfulness or argument.
Even asleep, life is
sweet. Imaginations sullen
with poverty and illness
are still imaginations. The third
finger slips into the
elastic fissure. Spring
brings zinnias to the
garden. Though refugees of
mental fight surrendered
unconditionally, they are
quilted against the cold
by polyester. If whoever stole
imagination's wealth
would give it back—
give red and gold
thread—their fingers
would embroider.

My tools as I think
them are perfect: ax bit
steel bright, square a Platonic
right angle, hammer head
substantially gleaming
with impact. Handles are
mortal. Hickory splits,
wedges loosen. The wood
itself sharpens this dream
of tools. Grain twists
from a tree's life
of wind and drought and
leaning for sunlight. I
follow the fibers that wander
like caverns. A knot
contorts splitting, but torched
by this toothed gleam
I come on this planed shape
askew but itself,
edged by a blue flame:
as if in the chimney's
soot throat
above kindling cedar.

The Morning After

As our President sleeps I see (in the dream
He cannot remember) industrial suburbs.
Petrochemical refineries isolate themselves in a glamour
Of lights by the Delaware, the James, the Savannah rivers.
Fumes fly like flags from catalytic towers.
Burnt stumps, half-extracted, rim strip mine cavaties.
Hard-hat men watch bulldozers consuming pastures,
Streams run mud like the aftermath of Gettysburg.
The meaning of this carnage of flattening and poisoning
Is these blocks with the family grocery closing,
These thin card houses to be swept away
And set up again by the car-blast of freeways.
The meaning of this sacrifice of clear running
Drink without metallic pollutants is the trail bike
For eleven-year-old boys, the reverberation
Of lawnmower engines against the brick walls
Of disused schools. The meaning of this poisoning
And dulling of the land is a poisoning and
Dulling of the mind, a satiety with televised
Violence and beer, a dull stupor of
Desire for desire like lava-colored underground
Coal fires eating their way toward our children.
Undetermined substances leach deeper into Love Canal.
The outgoing tide leaves mud flats mounded
With feces, dead birds coated with oil.
He smiles, asleep, his expression comforts,
He mouths unconsciously the names of our
Accomplishments, athletes and astronauts
Chewed with the bodies of Marines and underfed
Children in a saliva striped like the flag.

She

Billboards by Interstate Forty packed with giant
Cigarettes glisten her memory with clarinets
Plastered like organ pipes. The ducks in muddy
Ponds down banks shed flakes of her white.

She wrinkles in houses walled with round stones
Where magnolia leaves echo those ovals. She swings
Porch swings out of wind by potted geraniums,
Sings to eyes stone blind to print, alone.

She's advertised in clouds. The houses
Where she massages or dances her breasts
By rivers and golf courses are doused in bursts
Of gusts that hail her with ice for hours.

What if her eyes seem seeing, never seen?
Her flesh is comically bulging, available
As upholstery plump in Buicks and double
Under girdles. It fuels us like gasoline

With its sweat as of hoods streamlined with rain.
Maybe those lines that lean like veils
When clouds comb on the horizons seem forlorn.
Still, she's never wittier than in a storm.

She'll blow up your pants' legs like balloons.
Umbrellas will tumble and skirts show panty.
Shirts on lines will flap in a frenzy,
Flesh feel tingly and light, inflatable as tunes

You puff with your breath on party kazoos.
Animals will huddle and canter in their zoos,
As ladies in aprons gather cucumbers and radishes
From backyard gardens she so sweetly ravishes.

The Artesian Well

By the double lake left after the mining of gravel—
Through an iron stem—the overflow flowered.
It held its calyx to the stars and,
That moment, the sun. A sand grain
Rising as we knelt to drink
Came tumbling our psyches, blue as
The planet. Its drop held a face inside.
I had thrust it once into soil,
As it was planted once for me.
That water held our red clay ride
Over counties—our journey of begetting.
Our land had rubbed its broom sedge
And briars into the ecstatic
Undersides of our bodies.
Barbed wire strung by pastures
(As we moved together) had sharpened
Tension. Ground sloped
Upward and a thunderhead burst
Its column in rain. An egg
Of light had fertilized vision:
A blond boy walking a pasture.

The magnetic woods and all leaves
That lacerate sunlight like facets of ponds
Had centered their lines of force in us.
I'd passed on, as I had inherited,
The two-story dwelling with only six rooms
Under mansions of cloud.
The well by the Civil War house and
Spanish oaks broken by weather
Had raised its water to us and subsided.
We drank to our son on his wedding.

If you understand my accent,
You will know it is not out of ignorance.
Broom sedge in wind has curved this bent
Into speech. This clay of vowels, this diffidence

Of consonantal endings, murmurs *defeat*:
Caught like a chorus from family and servants.
This is the hum of blessings over the meat
Your cavalry spared us, echoed from an aunt's

Bleak pantry. This colorless tone, like flour
Patted onto the cheeks, is poor-white powder
To disguise the minstrel syllables lower
In our register, from a brownface river.

If it sounds as if minds were starved,
Maybe fatback and beans, yams and collards
Weighed down vitamins of wit, lard
Mired speed, left wetlip dullards

In cabins by cotton. But if bereft
Of the dollars and numbers, our land's whole
Breath stirs with Indian rivers. Our cleft
Palate waters for a smoke of the soul,

A pungence of pig the slaves learned
To burn in pits by the levee. This melon
Round of field and farmer, servant turned
Tenant, longs for a clear pronunciation,

But stutters the names of governors, Klan
And cross-burnings, mad dogs and lynchings.
So ours is the effacing slur of men
Ashamed to speak. We suffer dumb drenchings

Of honeysuckle odor, love for a brother
Race which below the skin is us, lust
Projected past ego onto this shadow-other.
So we are tongue-tied, divided, the first

To admit face to face our negligence
And ignorance of self: our musical tone
Of soul-syllable, penchant for the past tense,
Harelip contractions unable to be one.